BRITISH
RAILWAYS
48151

The World by Train

100 Legendary Railway Journeys

ROUGH GUIDES

The World by Train

100 Legendary Railway Journeys

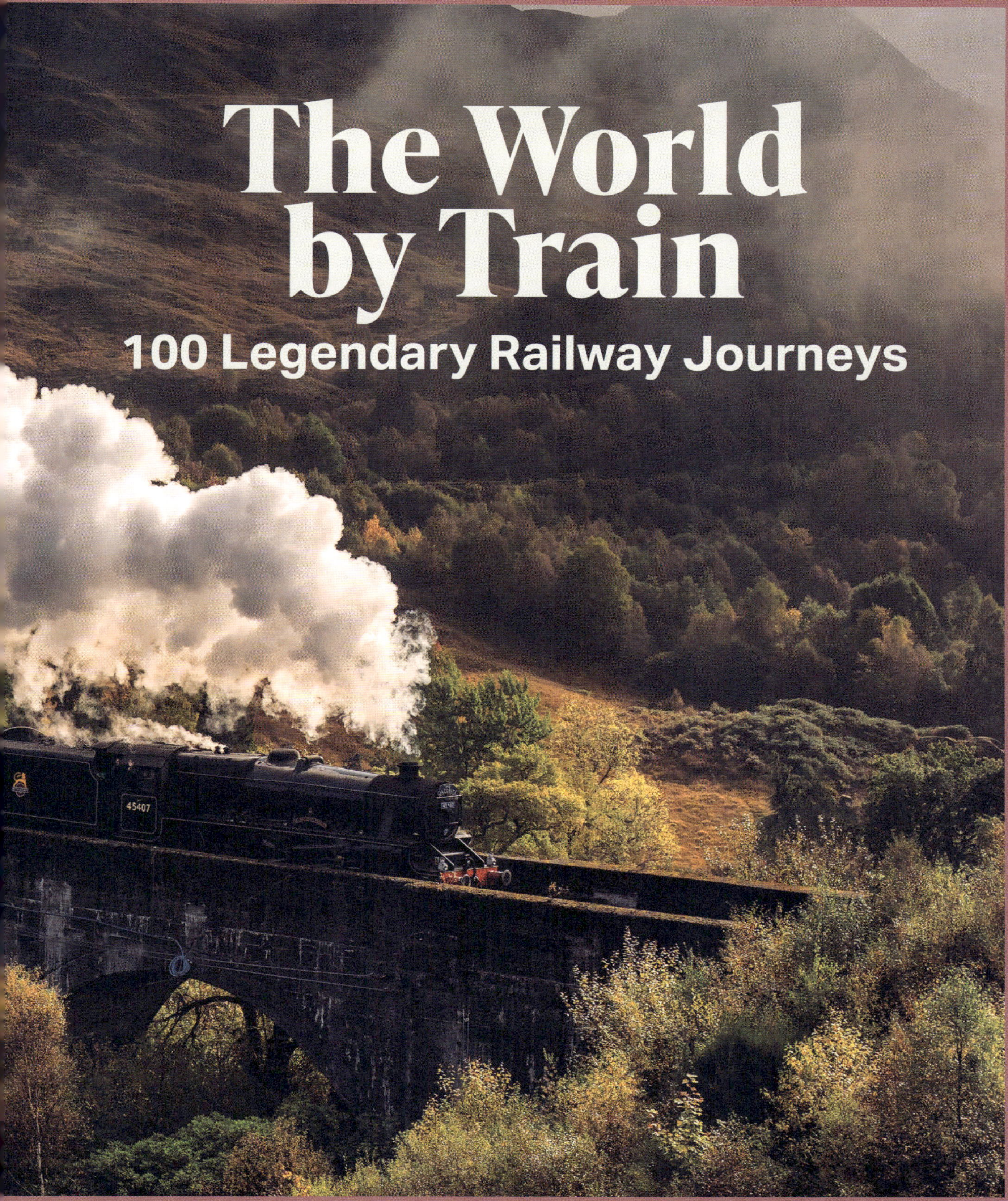

The World by Train

100 Legendary Railway Journeys

Introduction

The world looks different from a train window: cities slip into open country, mountains rise without warning and whole continents reveal themselves one journey at a time.

On the Beijing–Lhasa Railway, the line climbs onto the Tibetan Plateau past lakes, prayer flags and vast, treeless horizons. The Bernina Express makes the Alps feel theatrical, looping over stone viaducts and past glaciers before dropping towards Italy. In Norway, the Flåm Railway turns a short mountain descent into a sequence of waterfalls, tunnels and dark green fjord country, while The Ghan crosses Australia in a long, red sweep from one climate to another.

The 100 railway journeys in this book are legendary for many reasons. Some have glamour built into their name, like the Venice Simplon-Orient-Express or South Africa's Blue Train. Some are feats of speed and engineering, from the Tokyo–Kyoto Shinkansen to Morocco's Al Boraq. Others are memorable for smaller reasons: the hiss of steam on England's Bluebell Railway, salt air on Sri Lanka's Colombo–Galle coastal route or the glimpse of desert beyond the window between Khiva and Samarkand in Uzbekistan.

This is a book for travellers who like the idea of arrival, but love the pull of the journey more. Deserts, islands, glaciers, jungles, old imperial cities and remote mountain passes all have their part to play. What follows is an invitation to climb aboard.

PERURAIL

Great Alpine & Mountain Railways

Tracks climb where roads hesitate, edging through ravines before emerging into the clear expanse between serrated peaks. Rack lines grind towards snowy summits, threading through river-filled valleys. Some lines were built for miners, pilgrims or remote communities, others for early travellers in search of clean air and impossible views, but all share a sense of hard-won passage through landscapes that seem to resist the very idea of a railway.

Beijing–Lhasa Railway *CHINA*

(T) The Qinghai–Tibet railway section

If you're looking for a spectacular train journey, China's Beijing to Lhasa railway is an excellent choice. Not only is it the world's highest railway line, but it also boasts the highest altitude station and tunnel, too. The section from Xining to Lhasa, which covers nearly 2000km and takes 21 hours, passes through incredible scenery, much of it at altitudes higher than 4km – so high that the trains come equipped with oxygen masks in case passengers need them. Travellers can enjoy mountain, lakes and Tibetan grassland views as the train makes its way across the vast Tibetan Plateau, passing the shores of Qinghai Lake and the snow-capped peaks of the Tanggula Mountains. If the journey wasn't exciting enough, reaching Lhasa – a city with a mythical and deeply spiritual reputation – is a high point… in more ways than one.

Bernina Express *SWITZERLAND–ITALY*

The Bernina Express does something few trains manage: it carries you from the high Alps into Italy in a single, seamless journey. From St. Moritz the route climbs towards the Bernina Pass, passing Lago Bianco and the alpine landscapes around Ospizio Bernina before descending towards Tirano through a sequence of curves, viaducts and sudden changes in light. There is no rack assistance here, which makes the engineering feel all the more audacious, particularly on the long descent into the Val Poschiavo. In winter, the lake and pass can appear almost monochrome, while in summer the scenery softens into pasture, forest and terraced slopes. By the time the train reaches Tirano, the landscape, architecture and atmosphere have all changed. The high Alps are behind you, and you are, of course, now in Italy.

(L) The Bernina Express in Switzerland; (T) Views from the Red Train; (B) The Bernina Express travelling through Tirano

Centovalli Railway

SWITZERLAND–ITALY

The Centovalli Railway is a short journey with a crowded landscape. Running between Locarno and Domodossola, it threads through wooded ravines, stone hamlets, slender viaducts and deep streams that appear and vanish between tunnels. Compared with Switzerland's grander trains, the Centovalli feels almost intimate, brushing close to gardens and village roofs before swinging out above riverbeds or plunging into shadowed treelines. Locarno gives the route a relaxed lakeside start, with palms and Italianate squares, while Domodossola brings an Alpine borderland atmosphere at the gateway to northern Italy. Over its roughly 52km, the railway crosses dozens of bridges and tunnels, repeatedly climbing out of one narrow valley only to disappear into the next – a journey where the engineering is almost as striking as the scenery.

(O) View from Centovalli; (L) Camedo Station; (T) Domodossola Town; (B) Swiss hamlet of Intragna in Centovalli valley

Central Railway *PERU*

Ascending from the coastal humidity of Lima into the high Andes, the Central Railway of Peru climbs deep into some of the most difficult railway country in the world. The standard-gauge line was once the highest railway in the world, reaching 4,781 metres near Galera station. Its route is a remarkable feat of railway engineering, using a series of zig-zags, 69 tunnels and 58 bridges – including the famous Verrugas Bridge – to gain height through the mountains. As the urban sprawl of Lima disappears, the landscape changes dramatically, with steep valleys, barren slopes and mineral-rich peaks replacing the dry coastal plain. The higher the train climbs, the thinner the air becomes and the more remote the surroundings feel. By the time it reaches the high plateau, the railway has carried passengers from sea level into a stark Andean landscape of vast skies, rugged mountains and clouds far below.

(O) Central Andean Railway in the Andes; (L) The Verrugas Bridge; (R) Train carriages with windows in the roof

Cusco–Machu Picchu Railway *PERU*

The railway to Machu Picchu winds through the Urubamba Valley, following the river from the highlands around Cusco towards the warmer, greener slopes below. The scenery changes quickly along the way, from dry Andean hills and farmland to thick vegetation and cloud forest. The track follows the curves of the Vilcanota River, passing mountain villages, agricultural terraces and the remains of Inca settlements tucked into the valleysides. As the train descends, the mountains close in around the line, with steep cliffs and forested slopes rising on either side. Passengers can travel in the Pullman-style carriages of the Belmond Hiram Bingham or in the panoramic Vistadome, where large windows give a clear view of the surrounding landscape. The journey ends at Aguas Calientes, from where the road climbs towards Machu Picchu, but the changing landscape along the railway has already given a strong sense of the mountains and valleys that surround the famous site.

(O) The journey from Cusco to Machu Picchu through the Sacred Valley

Flåm Railway *NORWAY*

The Flåm Railway is best understood as a dramatic detour from the Bergen–Oslo line rather than a simple scenic add-on. From Myrdal, high on the main route between Bergen and Oslo, the branch drops steeply towards Flåm at the head of Aurlandsfjord, revealing a stunning spectacle. The line passes through tunnels, curves and mountain scenery at steep gradients that seem impossible for such a short journey. Waterfalls and valley walls press in close, while the change in climate and scale is immediate: from the bare upland railway around Myrdal to the green floor of the fjord country below. Though the journey is brief, and often busy in summer, the descent delivers the richness and variety of a much longer rail experience before ending at the edge of Aurlandsfjord, where mountains, waterfalls and deep, still water combine in one of Norway's defining landscapes.

(O & B) The train between Flåm and Myrdal; (T) The scenic village of Flåm

Glacier Express *SWITZERLAND*

(T) The Glacier Express from St. Moritz to Zermatt

The Glacier Express is famous for being slow, but the real point of this journey is how much of Switzerland it manages to encompass between Zermatt and St. Moritz. The route links Matterhorn country with Graubünden, crossing the Oberalp Pass and passing through a succession of valleys, bridges and tunnels where the landscape repeatedly resets itself. Chur gives the route a historic pause, the Landwasser Viaduct delivers one of Europe's most iconic railway scenes and the higher sections bring close-up views of bare rock, snowfields and alpine pastures. Along the way, the train follows the Rhine Gorge, where sheer cliffs rise above the river, before climbing through the Albula Valley towards St. Moritz. Rather than racing between destinations, the Glacier Express takes its time, meandering through the changing landscapes and revealing an extraordinary cross-section of the Swiss Alps in a single journey.

Jungfrau Railway *SWITZERLAND*

The Jungfrau Railway is one of Switzerland's great feats of mountain engineering, climbing from Kleine Scheidegg into the Eiger and on towards Jungfraujoch. The approach is memorable: restaurant terraces, walkers, cowbells and uninterrupted views of the Eiger, Mönch and Jungfrau. Then the atmosphere changes as the train disappears into the mountain, pausing at observation windows overlooking the north face of the Eiger before continuing to Jungfraujoch, Europe's highest railway station. The altitude is immediately apparent on arrival, where snow, ice and bare rock replace the green pastures and villages of the Bernese Oberland below. Few railways transform the landscape so completely, carrying passengers from pastoral Switzerland into a world of glaciers and high mountain wilderness in little more than an hour.

(O) Jungfrau Railway approaching Jungfraujoch; (T) From Jungfraujoch to Kleine Scheidegg; (B) Jungfrau Railway at Eiger Glacier Station

Mariazell Railway

AUSTRIA

The Mariazell Railway runs for 78km from St. Pölten into the mountains of Lower Austria. It was constructed to connect the provincial capital with Mariazell, an important pilgrimage destination, and its route follows the Erlauf valley before climbing into more rugged country around Gösing and the Ötscher massif. The railway passes through 19 tunnels and over 21 viaducts, with gradients and tight curves engineered into the narrow-gauge alignment to cope with the mountainous terrain. At Gösing, the line reaches around 890 metres above sea level, with views towards Ötscher, before continuing through the Erlauf Gorge and down towards Mariazell. Along the way, small stations and villages sit directly beside the track, while stretches of dense forest give way to open slopes and rocky mountain scenery. The final approach to Mariazell brings the railway into the town below its famous basilica, completing a journey that rises from the foothills around St. Pölten into the heart of the Austrian Alps.

(O) Himmelstreppe on the Mariazell Railway; (L) A signalman operates a traditional trackside points lever; (R) Mariazell Basilica

Mont-Blanc Express

FRANCE–SWITZERLAND

The Mont-Blanc Express links Martigny in Switzerland with Chamonix in France. From Martigny, the line climbs steeply through the Swiss Trient valley, using rack-rail sections to tackle the gradients as it passes villages, waterfalls and steep wooded slopes. At Le Châtelard it crosses into France, continuing through the narrow gorge and forests of the Chamonix valley before reaching Chamonix beneath the Mont Blanc massif. The railway was built to open up this part of the Alps to travellers and mountaineers, and its route still follows the contours of the original mountain railway rather than taking a direct line between the two towns. Along the Swiss section, the track repeatedly crosses bridges and clings to the valley sides, while the French approach opens out towards the peaks above Chamonix. The journey ends with Mont Blanc and the surrounding massif dominating the skyline, a fitting finish to a railway that spends much of its route squeezed between the valley floor and the mountainsides.

(O) Train from Chamonix to the Mer de Glace glacier; (L) Saint-Michel Church in the heart of Chamonix; (T) Mont-Blanc Express in autumn; (B) The original Chamonix Railway Station

Rauma Railway *NORWAY*

The Rauma Railway runs between Dombås and Åndalsnes, carrying passengers into some of Norway's most dramatic mountain scenery. Its best-known landmark is Trollveggen, the Troll Wall, Europe's tallest vertical rock face, which rises abruptly above the valley with an overwhelming sense of scale. Though the journey is relatively short, it packs in an extraordinary variety of scenery, following the Rauma River across graceful bridges and through narrow valleys before descending towards Åndalsnes. The railway remains constantly at the mercy of the landscape, threading its way through country where mountains, waterfalls and sheer rock faces dominate every view. Passing beneath the Troll Wall is the defining moment of the journey, where the sheer height and unbroken sweep of the cliff make the railway itself seem almost incidental within the landscape.

(O) Kylling Bridge; (T) Åndalsnes; (B) Troll Wall

Le Train Jaune *FRANCE*

Le Train Jaune is the French Pyrenees in bright, rattling miniature. This narrow-gauge mountain railway links with routes from Spain and crosses high country on a succession of lofty bridges, exposed ledges and sweeping curves that reveal ever-changing views across the valleys below. One of France's most distinctive regional railways, it climbs steadily through stone villages, open hillsides and rugged mountain scenery, its bright yellow carriages standing out against the landscape. In summer, the open-air carriages immerse passengers in the mountain landscape, with fresh air and uninterrupted views replacing the enclosure of a conventional train. Few railways offer such a continuous sense of height, carrying you across the Pyrenees on viaducts and mountainsides with the valleys always close at hand.

(O) Views from Le Train Jaune in winter; (T) Cassagne Bridge; (B) Passing through Villefranche-de-Conflent

Tren a las Nubes

ARGENTINA

The "Train to the Clouds" is one of the world's highest railways, climbing into the stark landscapes of northwest Argentina. Conceived in the early twentieth century as part of an ambitious rail link between Argentina and Chile, the line ascends gradually through the Andes by means of loops, zigzags and soaring viaducts, culminating at the spectacular La Polvorilla Viaduct, 4,220 metres above sea level. Now in use only as a tourist heritage railway, the portion of the line that passengers can travel on runs from San Antonio de las Cobres up to La Polvorilla, where the Argentinian flag is raised above the desert-like surrounds and visitors can browse for llama-wool scarves at the local Mercado Artesanal.

(O) Tren a las Nubes in Salta Province

W. P. & Y. R.
LIARD RIVER
TATSHESHINI RIVER

White Pass & Yukon Route Railway *ALASKA–CANADA*

Few railways capture the raw drama of the Klondike Gold Rush like the White Pass & Yukon Route Railway. Skagway sprang up almost overnight in 1897, a rough trading post for prospectors setting off on the 500-mile ordeal to Dawson City, and by 1900 the railway to Whitehorse had secured its survival. Today the ride is a far gentler encounter with the same fearsome country, following the gushing Skagway River past waterfalls, ice-packed gorges and steep rock walls before climbing towards the White Pass summit. The line shadows the old stampeders' routes through the Coast Mountains, where men once hauled a tonne of provisions through snow, avalanches and bitter cold. It is part mountain spectacle, part gold-rush time capsule, with Skagway's timber-fronted streets waiting at journey's end.

(O) White Pass & Yukon Route Railway in Skagway;
(L) Totem pole in Skagway; (R) An isolated part of the route

Wild Landscapes & Scenic Icons

Trains carve through places made for window seats: beneath mountain ranges, across Highland moors and alongside dramatic coastlines. Some routes are famous for a single unforgettable sight, others for the slow build of scenery over hours: dark forests opening onto lakes, vineyards giving way to mountains, white cliffs rising high above the sea. The pleasure lies in watching each landscape unfold gradually before yielding to the next.

Bergen–Oslo Railway

NORWAY

Almost as soon as the Oslo train leaves Bergen, it dives into the 7.6km Ulriken Tunnel and emerges at Arna, beginning one of Norway's great mountain rail journeys. Between Arna and Voss, the line is rarely far from the fjords, often clinging to narrow ledges blasted from the rock above the water. Tunnels, boathouses, birch woods and conifers rooted to steep crags define the landscape before the railway climbs steadily inland. At Myrdal, 866 metres above sea level, the railway seems to belong entirely to the mountains, its isolated station marking the junction with the Flåm Railway. Beyond lies the long climb to Finse, the highest station on the line, where snow sheds, windswept uplands and the Hardangerjøkulen ice cap announce the crossing of Norway's high plateau.

(O) Passing through the Hardangervidda National Park

California Zephyr *USA*

Running for more than 2,400 miles across the American West, the California Zephyr offers a remarkable view of the country's changing landscape. Departing the Midwestern plains of Chicago, the silver double-decker Superliner carries travellers through the heart of the Rockies and across the high deserts of Utah before descending into the greener valleys of Northern California. The railway tackles the steep Moffat Tunnel and the winding route through Glenwood Canyon, following the Colorado River through some of the most dramatic scenery of the journey. From the glass-walled observation car, the landscape changes from rolling prairies to the red-rock cliffs and canyons of the West. By the time the train reaches Emeryville, passengers have crossed a huge stretch of the American landscape, passing through plains, mountains and desert along the way.

(O) California Zephyr near Green River; (T) Chicago Union Station; (B) California Zephyr train

The Canadian

CANADA

Spanning the immense breadth of the second-largest country on earth. The Canadian is a legendary four-night odyssey that links the glass towers of Toronto with the Pacific shores of Vancouver. This transcontinental icon serves as a moving vantage, traversing the rugged, lake-strewn Canadian Shield and the seemingly infinite, golden horizons of the Prairie provinces. The journey's pinnacle is when it begins its dramatic ascent into the snow-capped Canadian Rockies, winding through high mountain passes and thick pine forests. What distinguishes this route is the profound sense of scale and isolation; from the stainless-steel dome of the Park Car, the transition from urban sprawl to raw, wilderness is both humbling and hypnotic. It remains the quintessential North American rail experience, a rhythmic, slow-motion passage that reveals the sheer, staggering magnitude of the Canadian landscape.

(O) The Canadian crossing Parry Sound, Ontario;
(L) Toronto city; (R) Downtown Vancouver

191
AMTRAK

Coast Starlight USA

Widely regarded as one of the great coastal journeys in North America, the Coast Starlight links the sprawling city of Los Angeles with the evergreen forests of Seattle. Over roughly thirty-five hours, the train travels through a remarkable variety of landscapes, following the Pacific coast past the beaches and cliffs of Southern California before turning inland towards the mountains of the Pacific Northwest. One moment you are looking out across the Pacific near Santa Barbara, and later watching the landscape change to dense forests and mountain valleys. The journey is anchored by the Sightseer Lounge, where floor-to-ceiling windows provide wide views of Mount Shasta, Klamath Falls and Upper Klamath Lake. By the time the train reaches Seattle, passengers have travelled through some of the most varied scenery along the West Coast, from beaches and coastal hills to forests, lakes and snow-capped mountains.

(O) Coast Starlight near Ventura, California; (T) View from the Amtrak Coast Starlight; (B) Amtrak observation car

Coastal Pacific *NEW ZEALAND*

(T) Coastal Pacific along the Pacific Coast, Canterbury

The Coastal Pacific weaves along the north-eastern edge of New Zealand's South Island between the port of Picton and the garden city of Christchurch. Over nearly 350km, the tracks are pinned between the rugged, salt-sprayed Kaikōura Ranges and the crashing turquoise breakers of the Pacific Ocean, often running so close to the shoreline that the surf feels within arm's reach. There is an evident feat of engineering as the train navigates narrow ledges and tunnels carved into the cliffside. Keep a keen eye on the rocky outcrops near the Ohau Point seal colony, where New Zealand fur seals are frequently seen basking in the sun on the rocks. As the train turns inland across the vast, connected rivers of the Canterbury Plains, it leaves behind it the remote, frontier beauty of the Southern Hemisphere's coastline.

Inlandsbanan *SWEDEN*

The Inlandsbanan runs north through Sweden's remote interior, linking small towns and villages across the country. Summer services run deep through the country's sparsely populated interior, passing endless conifer forests, mirror-like lakes, peat bogs and wide river valleys that seem to stretch without end. It is one of Scandinavia's most isolated railway lines, traversing landscapes where wilderness dominates and signs of habitation are few and far between. The train crosses the Arctic Circle en route to Lapland, where summer brings almost continuous daylight. North of the Circle, the line continues towards Gällivare, a gateway to the mountains and the wider landscapes of Swedish Lapland. The route passes through forests, wetlands and open fells, with long stretches where little interrupts the view from the train.

(O) Steel bridge at Storstupet; (T) Mora Railway; (B) Sign showing the crossing of the polar circle in Sweden

Kuranda Scenic Railway

AUSTRALIA

Rising from the tropical coastal plains of Cairns into the emerald-draped mountains of the Atherton Tablelands, the Kuranda Scenic Railway is a spectacular journey through a UNESCO World Heritage-listed rainforest. The line was built by labourers in the nineteenth century and meticulously carved by hand into the rugged McAlister Range. It comprises fifteen tunnels and 37 soaring bridges. From the vintage timber carriages, passengers can almost touch the dense ferns and towering palms of the jungle as the train winds upwards. The showstopper of the route occurs at the Barron Falls lookout, where the train pauses to allow travellers to witness the thunderous cascade plunging into the deep, mist-filled gorge below. This is the ultimate Australian rail experience, offering a slow, breathtaking passage into the heart of one of the oldest living rainforests on the planet.

(O) Kuranda Scenic Railway winding up the tracks;
(L, T & B) Kuranda Railway Station

ROCKY MOUNTAINEER
44.0
Danger
Private Property
No Trespassing
Trespassers will be
prosecuted
Police

Rocky Mountaineer

CANADA

The Rocky Mountaineer carves a spectacular path through the Canadian Rockies on a daylight-only journey, allowing passengers to see the mountains and valleys along the way. From Vancouver, the route follows the Fraser River through the steep walls of the Fraser Canyon before climbing into the Rockies, passing through historic tunnels and along the shores of mountain lakes. From the glass-domed GoldLeaf carriages, passengers have wide views of the peaks, forests and rivers outside, and wildlife such as bald eagles, elk and, occasionally, bears can be seen along the route. The combination of comfortable carriages and remote mountain scenery makes the journey one of the best ways to experience the Canadian Rockies by rail, with the changing landscape remaining the main attraction from beginning to end.

(O) Rocky Mountaineer in Alberta; (L) Mount Robson;
(R) Inside a GoldLeaf carriage on the Rocky Mountaineer

Tadami Line *JAPAN*

Some 270km north of Tokyo, Japan's Tadami Line spans 135km between Aizu-Wakamatsu Station and Koide Station in Uonuma City, following a breathtaking route through the Oku Aizu valley alongside the Tadami River. Depending on the season, passengers may see cherry blossom trees in full bloom, the stunning reds and oranges of autumn foliage, or find the landscape blanketed in snow. The line crosses several impressive bridges, allowing plenty of opportunities to catch sight of meandering rivers with a dramatic backdrop of snow-topped mountains. Much of the route winds through steep valleys and dense woodland, with the railway hugging the river as it passes through the remote countryside. At the Aizu-Wakamatsu end, visitors can explore the town's samurai history and Tsuruga Castle, while at Koide, in Uonuma City, they can see the rice fields and sample the region's famous Koshihikari rice.

(O) Ooshi Village views; (T) Train crossing the Tadami River Bridge, Japan; (B) Winter on the Tadami Line

TranzAlpine *NEW ZEALAND*

Often hailed as one of the world's most spectacular day trips, the TranzAlpine traverses the South Island of New Zealand, linking the flat Canterbury Plains of Christchurch with the rugged, rain-forested West Coast at Greymouth. The short journey is defined by its dramatic transition through the Southern Alps, where the train climbs to the high alpine settlement of Arthur's Pass before plunging through the five-mile-long Otira Tunnel. This route is an engineering marvel, featuring soaring viaducts like the Staircase, which spans deep, shingle-bottomed gorges carved by turquoise glacial meltwater. From the open-air viewing carriage, the landscape quickly shifts from the dry, tussock-clothed mountains of the east to the lush, ancient beech forests and misty river valleys of the west. This is an epic, high-altitude journey that perfectly captures the geological intensity and raw, untarnished beauty of the New Zealand wilderness.

(O) Passing through Arthur's Pass National Park; (T) New Zealand's Southern Alps; (B) Waimakariri Gorge

West Highland Line SCOTLAND

The West Highland Line takes its time leaving Glasgow before becoming one of Scotland's defining rail journeys. Loch Long, Loch Lomond and Rannoch Moor bring the first great shift in mood: mountains, pine and birch woods, open moor and remote stations, including Corrour, reached only by train or on foot. The extension to Mallaig is the real highlight: at Glenfinnan, the train curves over the 21 arches of the viaduct while the River Finnan runs towards Loch Shiel and the Jacobite monument stands below. Beyond it, Rum, Eigg and Muck appear offshore, followed by the white sands of Morar and Arisaig. On arrival at Mallaig, passengers are met by gulls, salt air and fishing boats, a world away from Queen Street Station.

(O) Glenfinnan Viaduct

Coast, Islands & Waterside Routes

Trains run close to the water here, where rails squeeze between rock and sea, follow broad rivers or slip inland towards ferry ports and island towns. The views shift quickly: terraced vineyards above the Douro, Mediterranean cliffs and coves, Corsican hills dropping to the coast's palm-fringed shorelines and fishing boats moored alongside the track. These are railway journeys shaped by tide, current and coast, with the water rarely far from sight.

Alicante–Dénia *SPAIN*

(T) TRAM d'Alacant service from Benidorm to Alicante passing Sierra Grosa

The Alicante–Dénia line is one of Spain's most rewarding coastal rail journeys, tracing the Costa Blanca north from Alicante towards the port city of Dénia. Part railway and part modern tram line, it travels at a leisurely pace through orchards, palm groves and seaside towns. Along the way, the line serves well-known resorts including Benidorm, Altea and Calpe, but also passes quieter stretches where rocky headlands drop towards small coves and fishing harbours. Mountains rise surprisingly close to the sea, particularly around Calpe and Altea, giving parts of the journey a much wilder backdrop than the Costa Blanca's resort-town reputation might suggest. The final stretch continues towards Dénia, where Montgó massif rises behind the town. By the time the train reaches the end of the line, passengers have seen the Costa Blanca unfold as far more than a succession of beaches: a varied landscape of mountains, farmland and busy Mediterranean communities.

Cairo–Aswan Route *EGYPT*

Taking the train through the heart of Egypt is one of the most rewarding ways to explore the Nile Valley. Departing from Cairo's imposing Art Deco Ramses Station, the railway follows the fertile ribbon of the Nile southwards through farmland, villages and palm groves to Luxor, Kom Ombo and Aswan. Along the way lie many of ancient Egypt's greatest monuments, including the temples of Luxor and Karnak, the Valley of the Kings and the Temple of Kom Ombo, while Abu Simbel is reached by road from Aswan. Several services operate between Cairo and Aswan, including comfortable overnight sleeper trains, making the railway a practical and atmospheric way to experience the landscapes and archaeological treasures of Upper Egypt.

(O) Travelling between the River Nile and Aswan;
(L) Traditional felucca sailing on the River Nile;
(R) The Great Temple of Abu Simbel

Cinque Terre Express *ITALY*

The Cinque Terre Line plays a thrilling game of hide and seek with the Ligurian coast, diving through tunnels before bursting into daylight above the turquoise sea. Between the elegant resorts east of Genoa and La Spezia's natural harbour, the track reveals tantalising glimpses of five villages wedged between steep hills and water. Their colourwashed houses rise in tight stacks above tiny harbours, while terraces and paths cling to the slopes overhead. Before the railway arrived, these settlements were virtually unknown beyond the region, and the line still feels like the most natural way to approach them. Monterosso al Mare provides one of the journey's classic arrivals, with the station set close to the shore. The views come in stages rather than a continuous panorama, which only heightens the anticipation each time the train races back towards the light.

(O) Manarola Railway Station; (T) Vernazza; (B) Manarola

Colombo–Galle line *SRI LANKA*

One of the most rewarding journeys on Sri Lanka's rail network is the line from Colombo to Galle, which follows the island's western coastline for much of its 130km route. Leaving the bustle of the capital behind, the train runs beside palm-fringed beaches, fishing villages, lagoons and broad stretches of sand, often so close to the Indian Ocean that waves seem only a few metres from the track. The journey takes less than three hours but reveals a coastline that changes gradually from busy suburbs to quieter seaside communities. Along the way, the train calls at Hikkaduwa, known for its beaches and coral reefs, and Ambalangoda, long associated with the carving of traditional wooden masks. The line ends at Galle, where the UNESCO-listed Dutch fort and its narrow streets recall the city's importance as one of the Indian Ocean's great colonial ports. Combining coastal scenery with historic towns and everyday local life, the railway offers one of the finest introductions to Sri Lanka's landscapes and cultural heritage.

(O) Train passing Katukurunda Beach; (T) Galle Fort; (B) Hikkaduwa Railway Station

Corsican Railway

FRANCE

Corsica's railway gives the island a remarkable inland dimension. The narrow-gauge network links Ajaccio, Bastia and Calvi across country that often feels too rugged for railways at all: mountains, deep gorges, pine forests and lofty bridges spanning rocky valleys. The route towards Corte is especially revealing, leaving the beaches and ports behind to enter the island's rugged interior, while the line to Calvi returns to a brighter coastal landscape of sandy bays and Mediterranean light. Crossing the dramatic Pont du Vecchio is one of the journey's defining moments, a striking feat of engineering suspended high above the river gorge. This is not a railway built for speed but for negotiating difficult terrain, with remote stations, steep gradients and an ever-present sense of the island's mountainous character.

(O) Eiffel Bridge over the Vecchio River

Derry–Coleraine Line

NORTHERN IRELAND

The Derry–Coleraine line is one of those everyday railways that quietly rivals far grander routes. Running along Northern Ireland's north coast, it combines broad estuaries, sweeping beaches and the ever-changing light of the Atlantic. The highlight comes near Mussenden Temple, where the railway skirts the shoreline beneath dramatic cliffs to create one of the most memorable rail settings in the British Isles. The line links the historic walled city of Derry with Coleraine and the Causeway Coast, passing long stretches of unspoilt sand and open sea. The route changes character with the seasons. In winter, dark seas and Atlantic storms emphasise the exposed nature of the coastline, while summer brings clear skies and long evenings that illuminate the beaches, cliffs and the iconic silhouette of Mussenden Temple. Few railways in the British Isles remain so consistently close to the sea.

(O) The north coast near Castlerock, Northern Ireland; (L) Mussenden Temple; (R) Derry–Coleraine Line running along the coast

Douro Valley Line *PORTUGAL*

The Douro Valley Line begins at Porto's magnificent São Bento station, completed in 1916 and lined with Jorge Colaço's celebrated blue-and-white azulejos. Leaving the city, the train dives through a succession of tunnels before emerging high above the Douro, where the Maria Pia Bridge and the Dom Luís I Bridge frame the river that will accompany the journey eastwards. After Livração, the line enters the valley's longest tunnel before descending towards Mosteirô, where broad views open across the water and terraced vineyards. East of Régua, the railway runs so close to the Douro that the view from the window is filled by little more than the river, its steep banks and the vineyards climbing above them. At Pinhão, one of Portugal's most attractive stations, painted *azulejo* panels celebrate the valley's wine-making traditions before the line continues towards Pocinho. The railway follows the Douro closely for much of its route, offering a continuous view of the river, valley and terraced vineyards.

(O) The Dom Luís I Bridge; (T) Railway viaduct in the Douro Valley; (B) Douro Valley

Konkan Railway *INDIA*

(T) Konkan Railway crossing the Zuari River, Goa

Threading south from Mumbai towards Goa and Kerala, the Konkan Railway opened up a coast that had long been awkward to navigate, cut as it is by rivers, creeks and estuaries. The reward is one of India's great slow-burn rail journeys, slipping in and out of view of empty beaches, coconut plantations, casuarina trees and the distant Western Ghats. It is useful as well as beautiful: daily express trains link Mumbai with Goa, while the line continues towards coastal Karnataka, where the run between Goa and Mangaluru is often described as among the most scenic routes in the country. The best stretches feel lush and amphibious, crossing palm- and mangrove-fringed waterways before dropping passengers within reach of places such as Ratnagiri, Gokarna and Udupi. Book ahead where possible – Konkan trains fill fast, and unreserved carriages can be punishingly crowded.

Southern Line *SOUTH AFRICA*

Hugging the shoreline of False Bay, the rail journey from Cape Town to Simon's Town is one of the world's most spectacular suburban railways. The route begins in the shadow of Table Mountain, passing through Cape Town's southern suburbs before reaching Muizenberg, where the track runs so close to the sea that waves can spray the windows. From here, the railway follows the curve of False Bay through the colourful seaside communities of St. James and Kalk Bay, passing beaches and small harbours with fishing boats pulled up along the shore. Passengers can look out across the bay towards the rugged mountains of the Cape Peninsula, with whales and Cape fur seals sometimes visible offshore. Beyond Fish Hoek, the line continues south towards Simon's Town, a historic naval base surrounded by steep hills and sheltered bays. For much of the journey, the railway and the sea seem almost inseparable, making this an unforgettable coastal ride as well as an essential part of everyday life on the Cape Peninsula.

(O) Glencairn on the coast to Simon's Town; (L) Muizenberg Station; (T) Kalk Bay Harbour; (B) St. James, Cape Town

Trenino Verde *ITALY*

Sardinia has two railway worlds: Trenitalia's standard-gauge network and the ARST-operated Trenino Verde (Little Green Train), whose narrow-gauge lines provide some of the island's most memorable journeys. The route between Cagliari and Arbatax is the longest on the system, climbing from the coastal plain into forests, uplands and remote mountain villages far removed from the island's resort beaches. Around San Girolamo, between Seui and Gairo, the railway passes close to the Montarbu Forest and the slopes of Monte Tonneri, where deer and mouflon inhabit one of Sardinia's richest natural landscapes. At Anulù, the highest station on the network at 865 metres, broad views open across the Seulo mountains before the line begins its long descent to the eastern coast. The Trenino Verde offers an intimate journey through the island's rugged interior, revealing landscapes largely untouched by modern development.

(O) The Trenino Verde in Lanusei; (L) Gairo Station; (R) The hill town of Seui

Deserts, Frontiers & Remote Railways

Rails, originally built for mineral extraction, empire expansion or simply survival, cross forests, desert, canyons and empty horizons. These are journeys through remote landscapes, where stations feel like outposts and the world widens with every mile. The appeal of these journeys lies in that frontier feeling: being carried, slowly and improbably, through country that has never been easy to cross and to places few people have dared to travel.

ALASKA

Alaska Railroad USA

Cutting through a vast, roadless wilderness that remains inaccessible to most, the Alaska Railroad offers a remarkable passage into the raw heart of the American North. Running from the coastal glaciers of Seward towards the interior city of Fairbanks, the railway connects two distinct routes through Anchorage: the Coastal Classic to Seward and the Denali Star to Fairbanks. The engineering is a testament to resilience, crossing the dizzying Hurricane Gulch trestle – suspended roughly 90 metres above the creek – and navigating the mountains of the Kenai Peninsula. From the glass-domed railcars, the landscape unfolds in dramatic succession: calving glaciers, braided rivers, and the immense, granite shoulders of Denali itself. What makes the railway distinctive is its role as a lifeline to remote communities, where passengers might spot moose, bears, or eagles from their seats, offering a vivid sense of the scale and wildness of Alaska.

(O) Denali Star train from Fairbanks to Denali National Park

El Chepe *MEXICO*

Plunging through the rugged heart of the Sierra Tarahumara, El Chepe provides a front-row seat to the staggering scale of Mexico's Copper Canyon – a labyrinth of ravines deeper and more expansive than the Grand Canyon. This engineering masterpiece, which took nearly ninety years to complete, connects the high-altitude plains of Chihuahua with the coastal lowlands of Los Mochis. The journey is defined by its sheer technical audacity, featuring 86 tunnels and 37 soaring bridges that stitch together a vertical landscape of pine-clad peaks and sub-tropical valleys. From the open vestibules, travellers can witness the dramatic transition in flora and climate as the train descends thousands of metres. Beyond the scenery, the route offers a rare window into the culture of the indigenous Rarámuri people, whose ancestral lands the tracks traverse, making it a profound narrative of survival and connection in one of the world's most difficult terrains.

(O) El Chepe, Barrancas del Cobre; (T) Valley of the Monks; (B) Stop signs at railway crossing

NR
75
THE GHAN
NR75

The Ghan *AUSTRALIA*

Bisecting the vast, scorched heart of the Australian continent, The Ghan is a legendary three-day journey linking the tropical north of Darwin with the temperate southern shores of Adelaide. The nearly 3,000km route carries travellers from the lush, humid Top End through the rust-coloured expanse of the Red Centre and into the outback beyond. Much of the journey is defined by its isolation, with ancient riverbeds, spinifex plains and the MacDonnell Ranges unfolding beyond the carriage windows. A stop in Alice Springs provides a chance to explore one of the outback's best-known settlements and learn more about its Aboriginal heritage and history. But it is the scale of the journey itself that makes The Ghan so memorable: mile after mile of desert, punctuated by the slow rhythm of the train and the changing colours of the Australian interior.

(O) The Ghan; (T) The Ghan train line crossing the Stuart Highway; (B) The Ghan in the Alice Springs Train Station

Grand Canyon Railway

USA

Steeped in the golden age of American travel, the Grand Canyon Railway offers a nostalgic, unhurried journey from the historic depot in Williams, Arizona, to the rim of one of the world's great natural landmarks. The journey is less about high-speed transit and more about the preservation of railway culture, featuring meticulously restored vintage carriages hauled by classic diesel or steam locomotives. As the train chuffs across the high-altitude ponderosa pine forests and the wide-open high-desert plateau, the experience is animated by Western-style musicians and tongue-in-cheek "train robberies" that evoke the frontier spirit of 1901. The flat, arid landscape gives no hint of the geological drama ahead until the train pulls into the 1910 log-style station at Grand Canyon Village. From there, the South Rim is only a short walk away, and the scale of the canyon makes a striking contrast with the quiet landscape crossed by the railway.

(O) Grand Canyon Railway; (L) Crossing railroad sign; (T) Vintage steam locomotive at the station in Grand Canyon Village; (B) Grand Canyon Village

Hejaz Railway

JORDAN

The Hejaz Railway in Jordan, which runs from South Amman into the desert, is one of the few surviving fragments of a much more ambitious line. Built by the Ottomans in the early twentieth century, the railway once stretched from Damascus in Syria to Medina in present-day Saudi Arabia. It was designed to dramatically cut the time needed for Muslim pilgrims to travel towards Mecca for the Hajj, while also strengthening Ottoman control over its distant Arabian provinces. During World War I, sections of the railway were repeatedly attacked by Arab forces. Following the collapse of the Ottoman Empire, much of the network fell into disuse, though the route through Jordan survived. Today, this delightful narrow-gauge line operates only sporadically, running special steam excursions – sometimes accompanied by live-action performances reenacting scenes from *Lawrence of Arabia*.

(O) Locomotive in Hejaz; (L) Camels walking the Hejaz Railway; (R) The abandoned station of Al-Hasa

The Iron Ore Train *MAURITANIA*

(O) Mauritania's Iron Ore Train crossing the remote Sahara Desert

The polar opposite of a luxury train, Mauritania's Iron Ore Train is for adventurous travellers only. Built in the 1960s, the rail line's principal purpose is the transportation of freight – specifically, iron ore, which is carried in open-top wagons through the Sahara from the mining town of Zouérat to the port city of Nouadhibou. Stretching for hundreds of kilometres across one of the world's most unforgiving landscapes, the train is among the longest and heaviest in regular operation. Passengers can use the train, but rather than travelling in a conventional carriage, some make the journey sitting directly on top of the ore in an open wagon, fully exposed to the desert climate. With blisteringly hot daytime temperatures, fine iron dust and often freezing nights, it is an extreme experience, but the endless dunes, vast empty horizons and extraordinary night skies make it one of the world's most unforgettable railway journeys.

Madaraka Express *KENYA*

Officially known as the Mombasa–Nairobi Standard Gauge Railway, the Madaraka Express links Kenya's Indian Ocean port city of Mombasa with the capital Nairobi. Financed largely through China's Belt and Road Initiative, the line opened to passengers in 2017, with freight services following soon after. The journey takes around six hours, crossing a changing landscape of coastal plains, savannah and highland country. Its defining moment comes as the train passes through Tsavo National Park, offering passengers a glimpse of safari from their seats. With plains stretching to the horizon, elephants and zebra sometimes visible from the carriage, and Mount Kilimanjaro appearing in the distance on clear days, few railway journeys offer such a spectacular window onto East Africa's wildlife and landscapes.

(O) Giraffes in Tsavo National Park; (T) Madaraka Express; (B) Mtito Andei Station

Namibia Safari Tour

NAMIBIA

Starting in Walvis Bay on Namibia's Atlantic coast and travelling nearly 4,000km to Pretoria in South Africa, the Namibia Safari is a 12-day journey through some of southern Africa's most remote landscapes. Leaving the coast, the train heads inland across the Namib Desert, following lonely tracks through immense expanses of sand, gravel plains and sparsely inhabited wilderness where settlements can be separated by hundreds of kilometres. Operated by Rovos Rail, the train provides luxurious sleeping suites with private bathrooms, elegant dining cars, a lounge and an open-air observation balcony, where passengers can watch the tracks stretch away across the desert, with little beyond sand, rock and distant mountains for miles around. Off-train excursions venture still deeper into Namibia's frontier landscapes, including the towering red dunes of Sossusvlei, wildlife-rich Etosha National Park and the vast Fish River Canyon, before the train continues south across the border into South Africa.

(O) A cheetah in the grasslands of the Kalahari Desert; (L) Oryx antelope in the Namib Desert; (T) Rovos Rail steam train; (B) A Rovos deluxe suite

Nordland Line NORWAY

Norway's Nordlandsbanen (Nordland Line) offers one of Europe's great long-distance railway journeys, running around 729km north from Trondheim to Bodø, the northernmost point reached by rail in Norway. Leaving the forests and valleys of central Norway behind, the line gradually enters a more remote landscape of mountain plateaus, deep valleys and Arctic wilderness. The journey's defining moment comes at Saltfjellet, where the train crosses the Arctic Circle, often marked by a celebratory whistle as passengers enter the land of the midnight sun. Beyond the crossing, the scenery becomes increasingly dramatic, with snow-capped peaks, glacial landscapes and isolated communities appearing along the route. Overnight services add another dimension to the experience, particularly around midsummer, when the sun dips towards the horizon but never fully disappears, leaving the landscape bathed in a surreal, endless twilight.

(O) Lønsdal Station; (T) Hell Station; (B) Mjelle Beach in Bodø

Pas–Churchill

CANADA

Forging a vital link through the subarctic expanse of northern Manitoba, the rail journey from The Pas to Churchill is one of Canada's most remote and evocative adventures. Known as the "Gateway to the North," The Pas marks the transition from the lake-dotted boreal forest into a landscape increasingly shaped by permafrost. The journey is defined by its sheer geological progression; from the vintage carriages, passengers witness the dense, green canopy of the forest gradually thin into the stunted trees and vast, frozen wetlands of the muskeg before finally giving way to the open, treeless tundra. As the only dry-land connection to the "Polar Bear Capital of the World," the route is a slow-motion epic where the sky takes on an immense scale, often illuminated by the Aurora Borealis. Arriving on the rocky shores of Hudson Bay, the journey stands as a testament to northern resilience, offering a rhythmic, multi-day passage into a wilderness where beluga whales and polar bears are among the only visible signs of life.

(O) Churchill Station in winter

Red Lizard Train *TUNISIA*

Tunisia's gorgeous Lézard Rouge (Red Lizard) train is a relic of the early twentieth century, a royal carriage built in France in 1910 for the beys of Tunis. Used by the ruling family before Tunisia's independence, the train later fell into disuse before being restored in the 1980s and returned to service as a tourist journey through the dramatic Selja Gorge. Departing from Métlaoui, the train follows a short but spectacular route between steep limestone cliffs, passing through a landscape of jagged rock formations, dry riverbeds and beautifully barren desert scenery. The gorge itself is the star of the journey, with its narrow passages and towering walls creating a striking contrast with the elegance of the carriage interiors. Decorated with polished wood, red upholstery and period details that inspired its name, the Lézard Rouge turns a brief mountain journey into a glimpse of Tunisia's royal past and rugged southern landscapes.

(O) The Red Lizard Train in Selja Gorges; (T) The Red Lizard Train; (B) View of the Selja Gorges from the train

Qinghai–Tibet Railway

CHINA

Climbing from the ancient city of Xining to the roof of the world, the Qinghai–Tibet Railway is one of the greatest engineering achievements of the modern era and the highest mainline railway on Earth. Crossing the vast Tibetan Plateau, the route traverses an extraordinary landscape of snow-capped mountains, frozen tundra and windswept grasslands, with more than 960km above 4,000 metres. The journey is defined by its immense altitude and breathtaking remoteness, passing herds of wild yak and Tibetan antelope before reaching the sacred city of Lhasa. Travelling across this high-altitude wilderness offers a profound sense of isolation and a rare perspective on one of the planet's most inhospitable yet spectacular frontiers, where cutting-edge engineering has forged a rail link through landscapes once considered beyond reach.

(O) Qinghai–Tibet Railway; (L) Mountain views from the carriage; (R) Xining Railway Station

TAZARA Railway

TANZANIA–ZAMBIA

One of Africa's longest railway lines, the TAZARA (Tanzania–Zambia Railway Authority) Railway links Dar es Salaam in Tanzania with Kapiri Mposhi in Zambia, crossing nearly 1,860km of varied landscapes. Built in the 1970s as a joint project between Tanzania, Zambia and China, the line was designed to give landlocked Zambia an independent route to the sea without relying on transport links through neighbouring countries under apartheid rule. Although the railway has historically carried mainly freight, especially copper exports, passenger services continue to operate with sleeper accommodation and dining facilities. The route crosses Tanzania's southern highlands, passing through remote valleys, forests and wildlife areas including Nyerere National Park, where passengers may catch glimpses of Africa's big-game landscapes from the train.

(O) The TAZARA Railway travelling through the hills of Tanzania's Mbeya Region; (L) Manze lake, Selous Game Reserve; (T & B) Leopards and hippos in Selous Game Reserve

Chepe
Chepe

สะพานโค้ง คสล.
ยาว ๘๗ ๓๐ ม.
สร้างเมื่อ
พ.ศ.๒๔๖๒

Cross-Country Journeys

These journeys call for long days, staring dreamingly out the window, leaving the city behind for river valleys, forests and mountains. Some cross the American interior, from the Adirondacks to the Southwest, while others cross Türkiye's Anatolian plateau or South Africa's interior. There is something satisfying about the slow accumulation of distance: breakfast in one landscape, dinner in another and the sense of travelling across the map in real time.

Adirondack *USA–CANADA*

(T) The Hudson River at Poughkeepsie, New York

Threading a picturesque path between the skyscrapers of Manhattan and the attractive shoreline suburbs of Montreal, the Adirondack is celebrated as one of North America's most beautiful day-long adventures. The journey is defined by its intimate relationship with water, tracing the eastern shore of the Hudson River Valley for hours before skirting the rugged, wild western edge of Lake Champlain. From the window, the landscape transforms from the historic estates of the Hudson Highlands into the dense, mountainous forests of the Adirondack Park, particularly breathtaking during the autumn when the foliage erupts in brilliant ochres and scarlets. What distinguishes this international route is its unhurried pace, allowing travellers to soak in the transition from the rolling vineyards and farmsteads of upstate New York to the quiet, frontier-like beauty of the Canadian border. It remains an evocative, cross-border classic that prioritises scenic immersion over speed.

Bangkok–Chiang Mai Sleeper Train *THAILAND*

The popular and often sold-out sleeper train linking Bangkok with Chiang Mai is one of Thailand's most atmospheric ways to travel between two of the country's most fascinating cities. Covering around 750km, the route passes the historic city of Ayutthaya, with its atmospheric temple ruins, before continuing north through changing landscapes of rice fields, rural villages and forested hills. As the train leaves the busy plains around Bangkok behind, the scenery becomes increasingly green and tranquil, offering a glimpse of everyday Thailand beyond the main tourist centres. Day services allow passengers to watch the countryside unfold from their seats, while overnight sleepers turn the journey itself into part of the experience, arriving in Chiang Mai ready to explore its temples, markets and the mountain trails of the surrounding region.

(O) Bangkok–Chiang Mai sleeper train passing through northern Thailand's forests; (L) Buddha statues at the entrance to Chiang Mai Railway Station; (T) Train hostess welcoming passengers at Hua Lamphong Railway Station; (B) Sleeping berths

Empire Builder *USA*

Following the route of early pioneers, the Empire Builder travels roughly 3,500km across the rugged northern United States, linking Chicago with the Pacific Northwest. The route sweeps across the golden, wind-scoured prairies of North Dakota before ascending into the dramatic, sawtooth peaks of the Montana Rockies. The journey's defining quality is its passage through Glacier National Park, where the tracks skirt the southern boundary, offering passengers unmatched views of ancient ice fields and turquoise alpine lakes. From the Sightseer Lounge, the transition from the vast "Big Sky" country to the misty, evergreen forests of the Cascade Range reveals the sheer diversity of the American north. Splitting at Spokane to reach either Seattle or Portland, the train remains a vita link across the continent, providing a rhythmic and authoritative perspective on the untamed scale of the wilderness.

(O) Amtrak Empire Builder in Skykomish; (T) North Fork Skykomish River; (B) Chicago Union Station

Indian Pacific

AUSTRALIA

Crossing Australia from Sydney to Perth, the Indian Pacific takes travellers across the heart of the continent, passing through some of the country's most striking and remote landscapes. The journey runs for more than 4,000km, beginning in the eucalyptus-covered hills and farmland of New South Wales before climbing through the Blue Mountains and heading west towards the dry plains of the Outback. The most memorable stretch comes across the Nullarbor, where the railway runs for hundreds of kilometres through an almost completely flat landscape of red earth, scrub and open sky. After crossing the vast interior, the scenery gradually changes as the train approaches Western Australia, with greener farmland and vineyards replacing the harshness of the desert. By the time it reaches Perth, passengers have travelled from Australia's east coast to its west, crossing an entire continent by rail.

(O) Passing through the Blue Mountains

Inverness–Kyle of Lochalsh SCOTLAND

The Inverness–Kyle of Lochalsh line crosses Scotland from the chilly waters of the east to the west coast opposite Skye. The railway was first opened as far as Strome Ferry in 1870, with the full 132km route to Kyle completed in 1897 after pressure from the newer West Highland Line. Leaving Inverness, the train follows the Moray Firth, where herons, swans, geese and bottlenose dolphins may be spotted, then crosses the Caledonian Canal before breaking away at Dingwall. Beyond Garve, Luichart, Auchuillin and Achanalt, the diesel train works towards Achnasheen, the route's highest station and a watershed between the Atlantic and the North Sea. Gaelic and Norse place names mark the way west, ending at Kyle of Lochalsh, the "Narrows of the Rolling Waves".

(O) Kyle of Lochalsh railway line at Attadale; (L) Moray Firth Headlands; (R) Eilean Donan Castle at Kyle of Lochalsh

Jungle Railway *MALAYSIA*

Stretching more than 500km across the interior of Peninsular Malaysia, the iconic Jungle Railway runs from Tumpat in the north to Gemas, linking the east coast with the country's main rail network. Taking its name from the dense jungle through which it passes, the route offers a slow and atmospheric journey through some of Malaysia's most remote landscapes, with opportunities to explore natural wonders such as the Gua Musang limestone cliffs and Jelawang Waterfall, as well as engineering landmarks like the Guillemard Bridge. Although spectacular, the Jungle Railway is not a fast route – the full journey takes more than 16 hours. As newer rail projects transform travel times across Malaysia, the Jungle Railway remains valued for the landscapes and communities it reveals along the way.

(O) Malaysia's Jungle Railway; (T) Guillemard Bridge; (B) Jelawang Waterfall

Lake Van Express *TÜRKIYE*

Evocatively named the Lake Van Express, the Ankara–Tatvan train offers an epic long-distance journey through the heart of Türkiye. Beginning in the capital, Ankara, the train heads east for more than 1,350km until it reaches Tatvan on the western shores of Lake Van. Taking around 26 hours, the journey crosses the vast Anatolian plateau, passing farmland, remote towns and increasingly rugged mountain country as the train makes its way into eastern Türkiye. Much of the pleasure comes from simply watching this enormous landscape change outside the window, particularly as daylight fades over the mountains and passengers settle into their sleeping compartments for the night. It has become one of Türkiye's best-known rail trips, with many passengers continuing from Tatvan to explore Lake Van and the centuries-old Armenian churches scattered around its shores and islands.

(O) Akdamar Island on Lake Van; (L) Lake Van Express; (R) Lake Van

Reunification Express

VIETNAM

The railway running north to south through Vietnam is unofficially known as the Reunification Express, a reference to the line's symbolic role in reconnecting Hanoi and Ho Chi Minh City after the division of North and South Vietnam. Stretching 1,726km along much of the country's coastline, the route takes around 30–36 hours and reveals a remarkable variety of landscapes, from rice fields and fishing villages to mountains, beaches and tropical countryside. Among the highlights are the dramatic Hải Vân Pass, where the railway clings to the mountains above the coast, and the historic city of Huế, once the imperial capital of Vietnam. Although it is not a luxury train, the Reunification Express offers one of the most rewarding ways to experience the country, travelling at a slower pace and bringing passengers close to the landscapes and communities along the way.

(O) Hải Vân Pass; (L) Notre-Dame Cathedral Basilica of Saigon; (T) Imperial City of Huế; (B) The Húc Bridge on Hoàn Kiếm Lake, Hanoi

Southwest Chief *USA*

Steeped in the lore of the American West, the Southwest Chief charts a legendary 3,540km course from the skyscrapers of Chicago to the palm-fringed boulevards of Los Angeles. This route follows the historic path of the Santa Fe Trail, cutting a rhythmic path across eight states and some of the most iconic topography in the United States. The journey is defined by its transition into the high desert, where the rolling prairies of the Midwest give way to the red-rock mesas of New Mexico and the stark, sun-bleached beauty of the Mojave Desert. From the glass-walled observation car, the scale of the landscape is staggering, particularly as the train climbs over the 2,313m Raton Pass on the Colorado-New Mexico border. It remains an excellent way to experience several states in one journey and witness the wild landscapes of the American Southwest.

(O) Amtrak Southwest Chief Train; (T) Red rock cliffs in Walatowa, Jemez Pueblo; (B) Joshua Trees in the Mojave Desert

Vitória–Minas Railway

BRAZIL

Linking the Atlantic coast at Vitória to the iron-rich heartlands of Belo Horizonte, the Vitória–Minas Railway offers a rare glimpse into the industrious soul of Brazil. As the train pulls away from the ocean, the journey transforms into a moving tapestry of the state of Minas Gerais, rolling through deep river valleys and past the rugged, mineral-laden peaks that have shaped the region's history. While the route is a vital artery for the country's mining industry, the passenger experience is defined by a gentle, unhurried rhythm that invites observation of daily life at rural stations and the changing tropical terrain. The true magic lies in the transition from the humid coastal air to the cooler, mountainous interior, providing a front-row observation of the country's vast scale, natural resources and its people.

(O) Coastal city of Vitória; (L) Iron ore mine in Minas Gerais; (R) Restaurant car of the Vale SA passenger train

High-Speed & Modern Rail Icons

Speed changes the character of a journey, turning distances into effortless connections. These routes belong to the modern railway age: Japan's Shinkansen sweeping past Mount Fuji, European high-speed trains linking cities and stations of glass and steel. The thrill lies not only in velocity but in precision – the confidence of a train that departs on time, gathers speed smoothly and makes journeys once measured in days feel remarkably close.

11
10
9
8
7

Al Boraq

MOROCCO

Morocco's Al Boraq represents one of the most significant steps forward in African rail travel: the continent's first high-speed passenger service. Opened in 2018, the line connects Tangier with Casablanca, cutting across the Atlantic coastal plains at speeds of up to 320 km/h. From its sleek modern carriages, the landscape shifts rapidly between whitewashed towns, farmland, olive groves and the expanding urban corridors of northern Morocco. Beyond its speed, Al Boraq represents a broader transformation of Moroccan transport, bringing major cities closer together and introducing a new era of rail travel to the continent. It is a striking example of how high-speed rail can reshape the experience of distance, turning journeys that once took hours longer into seamless connections between Morocco's economic and cultural centres.

(O) Al Boraq high-speed trains in Tangier Railway Station

Beijing–Shanghai High-Speed Railway *CHINA*

Services along the Beijing–Shanghai High-Speed Railway are the fastest scheduled trains in the world, allowing passengers to travel the 1,320km between Beijing and Shanghai in an astonishing 4 hours 20 minutes. Beginning at the Beijing South station, the route heads south, making stops at major Chinese cities – including Nanjing and Suzhou – before reaching Shanghai's Hongqiao Station. It's a popular train, with more than 500,000 people thought to use at least a section of the route every day, making it one of the busiest and most important rail links in China. Joining them for the full length is the perfect way to travel between Beijing and Shanghai: it's just as quick as flying (and far less hassle), and offers a perfect opportunity to see the country zipping past from the comfort of your seat, while experiencing one of China's most impressive feats of modern engineering.

(O) CR400AF Fuxing high-speed train at Beijing South Railway Station; (L) Railway porter at Beijing South Railway Station; (T) Train conductor; (B) Beijing–Shanghai High-Speed Railway

Gotthard Panorama Express *SWITZERLAND*

The Gotthard Panorama Express turns the classic north–south crossing of Switzerland into a journey of contrasts, combining a lake voyage, historic railway and dramatic Alpine scenery. The journey begins by the water, taking the route from Luzern to Flüelen, where paddle steamers still cross Lake Lucerne. From there, the railway follows the historic Gotthard line towards the Italian-speaking south, revealing views of the Urner See, the Reuss valley and the remarkable engineering that carved a route through the mountains. This corridor has always carried much more than tourists, with passenger and freight trains sharing one of Switzerland's most important links to Italy. The highlight of the route is the gradual shift into Ticino: the light becomes warmer, German station names give way to Italian, and towns such as Bellinzona sit beneath castles that recall the strategic importance of this Alpine passage.

(O) Express train on the old Gotthard Railway;
(L) Airolo Railway Station; (R) The Gotthard Panorama Express

8车 C97 10排-01排
琅勃拉邦→万象
LCR
KZ 040508

Kunming–Vientiane Railway

CHINA–LAOS

The China–Laos Railway opened in 2021, creating the first modern railway connection between Laos and China and transforming travel through one of Southeast Asia's most mountainous countries. Running between Kunming in southern China and Vientiane, the line cuts through dramatic terrain with long tunnels, major bridges and steep valleys that made construction a formidable engineering challenge. Although much of the route passes underground, the occasional glimpses of forested mountains and rugged landscapes reveal the scale of the terrain being crossed. Within Laos, the railway has dramatically reduced journey times, linking Vientiane with popular destinations such as Luang Prabang and Vang Vieng and offering a faster, more comfortable alternative to road travel. More than simply a transport link, it represents a new connection between southern China and mainland Southeast Asia.

(O) The high-speed train about to depart for Vientiane

renfe
AVE
renfe
AVE
10
POR FAVOR, MANTENGA LA DISTANCIA DE SEGURIDAD

Madrid–Seville AVE *SPAIN*

The Madrid–Seville AVE transformed Spanish rail travel. Opened in 1992 as part of the country's drive to modernise ahead of Expo '92, Spain's first high-speed line linked the capital with Seville in just a few hours, replacing a much slower rail journey between the two cities. The AVE, whose name means "bird" in Spanish, introduced a new era of speed and efficiency, with trains capable of reaching 300 km/h. From Madrid, the line heads south through the dry plains of Castilla-La Mancha before reaching Córdoba, where the Mezquita provides one of the journey's great cultural highlights. Beyond Córdoba, the landscape becomes lush and greener as the railway crosses Andalucía towards Seville and its distinctive skyline of tiled rooftops, the Giralda and the towers of Plaza de España.

(O) AVE high-speed train at Santa Justa Station, Seville;
(T) Travelling through the Spanish countryside; (B) Sevilla Santa Justa Station

Paris–Lyon TGV *FRANCE*

The Paris–Lyon TGV route changed the future of rail travel when it opened in 1981, becoming France's first dedicated high-speed railway and the model for a new generation of fast trains around the world. Linking the capital with France's second-largest city, the line cut journey times dramatically and introduced the now-iconic orange TGV trains to the public. Built across the rolling landscapes of Burgundy, the route was designed around speed and efficiency, allowing trains to reach 260km/h at launch and later much higher speeds. The Paris–Lyon line changed how Europe viewed distance, proving that rail could compete with air travel while offering a smoother city-centre-to-city-centre connection. Its success laid the foundation for France's expanding TGV network and helped inspire the high-speed rail revolution that followed across Europe and beyond.

(O) The Sud-Est Line; (T) Viaduct in Burgundy; (B) Gare de Lyon-Part-Dieu

21
KYUSHU
WEST JAPAN

Shinkansen *JAPAN*

For many visitors, the ride from Tokyo to Kyoto is the ultimate Japanese rail journey: fast, polished and thrilling. The Tōkaidō Shinkansen runs west from the capital through Nagoya to Kyoto and Osaka, forming the busiest and most famous section of Japan's high-speed rail network. Since opening in 1964, it has become a symbol of Japanese precision, combining remarkable speed with a reputation for safety and punctuality. The experience is almost deceptively smooth, as the old Tōkaidō corridor flickers past in a blur of suburbs, fields and industrial towns. On clear days, Mount Fuji appears beside the route near Shin-Fuji Station, rising above the landscape as one of the journey's defining sights. At the other end waits Kyoto, Japan's ancient capital, a modern city filled with temples, shrines, gardens and historic districts that provide a striking contrast to the futuristic train that brought you there.

(O) N700 Series Shinkansen awaiting departure at Kyoto Station; (L) Shinkansen in Tokyo; (R) Kyoto Station

N700

Heritage, Steam & Narrow-Gauge Railways

Steam changes the rhythm of a journey, slowing to the pace of gradients and curves. These routes belong to an older world: the Bluebell Railway threading through the English countryside, the Darjeeling Himalayan Railway climbing into the clouds, the Durango & Silverton following a wild canyon. Nostalgia is only part of the experience: there is also the sound of steam, the changing scenery and the pleasure of travelling on a railway built for another era.

Bluebell Railway *ENGLAND*

Vintage steam locomotives still chuff through the High Weald on the Bluebell Railway, running eleven miles from Sheffield Park to East Grinstead via Horsted Keynes and Kingscote. The stations have been beautifully restored in keeping with the period in which they were built, and Sheffield Park has railway sheds and a small museum. There is a touch of childhood nostalgia, too: Stepney, one of the railway's real steam locomotives, became a character in *Thomas the Tank Engine*. Sheffield Park itself makes a fine southern terminus, with Capability Brown's landscaped gardens close by, brimming with lakes, waterfalls and seasonal colour. The Bluebell is less about covering distance than about enjoying a carefully preserved railway that connects passengers to the gentle hills, sunken lanes and villages of the High Weald.

(O) The Bluebell Railway at Horsted Keynes Station

Darjeeling Himalayan Railway *INDIA*

The UNESCO-listed narrow-gauge Darjeeling Himalayan Railway – popularly known as the "Toy Train" – was completed in 1881 and remains one of the world's most remarkable mountain railways. Starting from New Jalpaiguri, the line climbs more than 2,000m into the foothills of the Himalayas, using tight curves, loops and steep gradients to gain altitude on its way to Darjeeling. For much of the route, the tracks run alongside the road and squeeze through busy towns and villages, passing remarkably close to houses, shops and market stalls. The most dramatic section comes around Ghoom, the highest station on the route, and the nearby Batasia Loop, where the railway curls around itself to negotiate the steep terrain and, on clear days, opens up views towards the snow-capped Kanchenjunga Range. Regular services still operate alongside heritage runs hauled by the railway's steam locomotives, carrying passengers past tea plantations, Buddhist monasteries and the densely settled slopes around Darjeeling.

(O) Darjeeling Toy Train navigating the Batasia Loop; (L) Coal being fed into a Darjeeling Himalayan Railway steam locomotive; (T) Darjeeling Himalayan Railway; (B) Japanese World Peace Pagoda in Darjeeling

Diakopto–Kalavryta Rack Railway *GREECE*

The Diakopto–Kalavryta Rack Railway, also known as the Odontotos, is one of Greece's most dramatic short rail journeys, climbing from the Gulf of Corinth into the mountains of the Peloponnese. Built in the late nineteenth century, the line uses rack sections to overcome steep gradients as it winds through the Vouraikos Gorge, where sheer rock walls, bridges, tunnels and narrow ledges reveal the skill behind its construction. At the top, Kalavryta offers a mountain setting of fir forests and cool air, while also carrying the memory of its important wartime history. From the coastal town of Diakopto to the highlands above, the short journey delivers a striking change of scenery, moving from the blue waters of the Gulf of Corinth into a dramatic mountain landscape.

(O) Odontotos Rack Railway; (L) Rack Railway under the Helmos Mountain; (R) View from the driver train cab

Durango & Silverton Narrow Gauge Railroad USA

Winding through the remote wilderness of the San Juan National Forest, the Durango & Silverton Narrow Gauge Railroad is a living time capsule of the American frontier. Originally built in 1882 to transport silver and gold ore, the line remains a narrow-gauge marvel, its tracks measuring just three feet apart to navigate the sharp curves of the Animas River Canyon. The journey is defined by its dramatic shelf-hugging stretches, where the coal-fired steam locomotive clings to sheer granite cliffs hundreds of feet above the churning white water. As the train chuffs from the historic depot in Durango to the high-altitude mining town of Silverton, the landscape changes from lush meadows to rugged alpine country where roads are few. The soot, the rhythmic whistle, and the smell of woodsmoke offer an evocative, visceral connection to nineteenth-century engineering, making this one of the most atmospheric mountain passages in North America.

(O) Steam engine train travelling from Durango to Silverton through the San Juan Mountains in Colorado

Ffestiniog & Welsh Highland Railway *WALES*

One of the oldest surviving railways in the world, the Ffestiniog and Welsh Highlands Railway operates a number of scenic routes throughout Wales' Snowdonia National Park. With a fleet of thirty heritage locomotives, some of which date back to the 1860s, the railway offers trips linking the mining town of Blaenau Ffestiniog with the port of Porthmadog and the imposing thirteenth-century castle at Caernarfon, all of which trundle on narrow-gauge lines through the dramatic scenery of North Wales. Perhaps the most enjoyable outing is the Caernarfon–Beddgelert journey, a full-day excursion through lush mountain valleys, past sparkling lakes and beneath the shadow of Snowdon itself, with the line winding through some of the most spectacular scenery in the national park.

(O & L) Steam trains on the Welsh Highland Railway;
(T) Interior of a steam locomotive firebox; (B) Rhyd Ddu Station

Fianarantsoa–Côte Est (FCE) *MADAGASCAR*

The Fianarantsoa–Côte Est – an isolated railway linking the inland city of Fianarantsoa with the port of Manakara – is a slow but hugely enjoyable journey through the varied landscapes of southeast Madagascar. Starting at an elevation of around 1,100 m, the train descends through the highlands, passing rice paddies, forests, villages and steep valleys before eventually reaching the coast. Along the way, the line crosses numerous bridges and winds through tunnels, negotiating terrain that makes road travel difficult. Used primarily by local passengers to transport people and goods, the train can be busy with traders carrying fruit, vegetables and other produce, giving the journey a lively, distinctly local character. One of its most unusual moments comes near Manakara, where the railway crosses the runway of the local airport before continuing towards the Indian Ocean.

(O) Travelling through Fianarantsoa; (L) Fianarantsoa Railway Station; (T) Buying and selling produce en route is common; (B) The old town of Fianarantsoa

Kalka–Shimla Railway *INDIA*

In the nineteenth century, the hill station of Shimla became the summer capital of British India, creating a need for a reliable railway connection to the fashionable but difficult-to-reach city. The Kalka–Shimla Railway, after years of planning and construction, finally opened in 1903. The 96km narrow-gauge line climbs steeply into the Himalayas, crossing numerous bridges and passing through more than 100 tunnels as it winds from Kalka to Shimla. The scenery becomes increasingly dramatic as the train rises through pine forests, deep valleys and mountain slopes. Look out for the railway's distinctive token system, in which staff exchange physical tokens to authorise trains to enter single-track sections, a simple but ingenious system that helps prevent two trains from occupying the same section at once.

(O) Train passing through a tunnel on the Kalka–Shimla Railway; (T) City of Shimla; (B) Station stop

S R

Nilgiri Mountain Railway

INDIA

The narrow-gauge Nilgiri Mountain Railway links the Tamil Nadu town of Mettupalayam with the hill station of Udhagamandalam (Ooty), climbing around 1,850m over a short 46km journey. Along the way, it passes through sixteen tunnels, eleven stations and nineteen bridges as it winds into the Nilgiri Hills. Its defining feature is the Abt rack-and-pinion system, used on the steepest sections to help the trains climb gradients that would be impossible for a conventional railway. The lower section between Mettupalayam and Coonoor is still worked by steam locomotives on scheduled services, adding another layer of historical character to the journey. Beyond the engineering, the railway is a spectacular way to enter the hills, climbing through forests and tea plantations and along the dramatic Hulikal ravine.

(O) Nilgiri Mountain Railway was built in 1908 and still uses original locomotives; (L) Monkey stopping for a snack on the railway in Nilgiri; (R) The train entering a tunnel cut right into the mountains

Ōigawa Railway *JAPAN*

The Ōigawa Railway, based in the city of Shimada, is unashamedly retro. Running a fleet of four 1930s steam trains and two mid-twentieth century electric locomotives, all of which pull carriages dating back to the 1950s, the line easily evokes the feeling of travelling in a bygone rail era. It's a line primarily aimed at tourists, with the route starting at Kanaya station and trundling up through the attractive Ōigawa river valley, calling at stations where passengers can alight and make use of the hot springs or go hiking in the splendid Southern Alps National Park. As an extra treat, the Ōigawa line also frequently runs *Thomas the Tank Engine* excursions, a nostalgic nod to the popular British children's television series from the 1980s.

(O, T & B) Thomas the Tank Engine steam locomotive

BRITISH
RAILWAYS
48151

Settle–Carlisle Line *ENGLAND*

The Settle–Carlisle line is one of Britain's great surviving railway journeys, crossing the Pennines between Yorkshire and the border city of Carlisle. Built by the Midland Railway in the late nineteenth century, it passes through some of northern England's most distinctive upland country and survived several attempts to close the route in the twentieth century. Its most iconic landmark is Ribblehead Viaduct, while the rest of the journey unfolds through wide moors, stone walls, restored stations and long gradients. Further north, Appleby comes into view with its twelfth-century castle, before the line descends through woodland around Lazonby and Kirkoswald and follows the River Eden towards Carlisle. Shaped by centuries of cross-border conflict, Carlisle brings the journey to a fitting close, with its castle and museums within easy reach of the station.

(O) Stanier Class 8F steam locomotive; (T) Along the Settle to Carlisle Railway; (B) Ribblehead Viaduct

Cultural Routes & Slow Travel

Some journeys are best taken at a relaxed pace, where the pauses are as meaningful as the miles covered. These routes follow old trading paths, mountain railways and revived local lines, linking landscapes with the towns and traditions that shaped them. From Sri Lanka's hill country to the Silk Road cities of Uzbekistan, Japan's mountain railways and the return of rail to Northumberland, they leave time to explore historic stations, local markets and everyday life.

Dresden–Prague *GERMANY–CZECHIA*

(T) EuroExpress passenger train to Prague

Dresden–Prague is one of the great river-border journeys of Central Europe, following the Elbe out of Saxony and into Bohemia. Dresden is a city of major historical interest, with the Zwinger, Semperoper and Frauenkirche among its great sights, while Prague needs little introduction, with its castle, Charles Bridge, Old Town Square and the narrow streets of Malá Strana. Between them, the railway gives the journey its texture, running beside the Elbe through the sandstone cliffs and wooded hills of Saxon and Bohemian Switzerland before entering the wider valley around Děčín and Ústí nad Labem. Villages, riverside towns and wooded slopes appear between stretches of rock and forest, following an old cultural corridor between Germany and the Czech lands. At Děčín, the railway crosses the river and passes beneath the castle before continuing south through the Elbe valley towards Prague.

Kandy–Ella Line *SRI LANKA*

The railway from Kandy to Ella cuts through the heart of Sri Lanka's tea country, climbing into the central highlands through plantation towns, quiet stations and mist-covered hills where the track seems perfectly matched to the landscape. Along the way are landmarks such as the Nine Arch Bridge and the famous Demodara Loop, where the railway spirals through a tunnel before crossing beneath itself. The journey is shaped as much by its atmosphere as its scenery, with open carriage doors, tea pickers at work, station vendors and endless tea estates creating a vivid sense of travelling through rural Sri Lanka. As the train climbs higher, the views open across rolling plantations and forested valleys, while the slow pace allows passengers to take in the changing landscape. It is this combination of scenery, everyday life and the character of the railway itself that makes the journey from Kandy to Ella a memorable and unique way to experience Sri Lanka.

(O) Railway between Kandy and Ella through Sri Lanka's hill country

Khiva *TO* Samarkand

UZBEKISTAN

For centuries, merchants crossing the Kyzylkum Desert between the Silk Road cities of Khiva, Bukhara and Samarkand faced long and arduous journeys by camel caravan, often taking days to complete. Today, Uzbekistan's modern high-speed railway covers the same broad route in a matter of hours, transforming one of Central Asia's great historic trading corridors into an accessible and comfortable rail journey. Along the way lie some of the Islamic world's finest architectural treasures, from the UNESCO-listed Registan in Samarkand to the richly tiled mosques and madrassahs of Bukhara and the remarkably preserved walled city of Khiva. Travelling by rail provides a fitting way to connect these remarkable cities, following a route that has carried merchants, scholars and travellers between Central Asia and the wider world for centuries.

(O) Uzbek couple in traditional dress, Bukhara; (L) Shah-i-Zinda complex in Samarkand; (R) High-speed train in Uzbekistan

Kurobe Gorge Railway *JAPAN*

(T) Kurobe Gorge Railway looks spectacular in autumn

The Kurobe Gorge Railway is one of Japan's most dramatic mountain railways, following the Kurobe River deep into the Northern Japan Alps. Running for roughly 20km between Unazuki and Keyakidaira, this narrow-gauge line winds through a steep V-shaped valley crossed by lofty bridges and densely forested slopes. Most carriages are open-sided, bringing the rushing river and surrounding mountains remarkably close, with the best views on the right-hand side when travelling from Unazuki. The railway forms part of the Tateyama Kurobe Alpine Route and Kurobe-Unazuki Canyon Route, but it is equally rewarding as a return journey in its own right. Along the way, stations provide access to hiking trails and hot springs, while autumn transforms the valley into one of Japan's finest displays of seasonal colour.

Lindau–Innsbruck

GERMANY–AUSTRIA

The Lindau–Innsbruck route begins on Lake Constance, close to the meeting point of Germany, Austria and Switzerland. From Lindau, set on an island linked to the mainland by a causeway, the railway follows the lakeshore into Austria and Bregenz, home to the Bregenz Festival and its famous floating stage on Lake Constance. Beyond Dornbirn and Feldkirch, the line continues through Vorarlberg to Bludenz, where the yellow Montafonerbahn railcars branch off for Schruns. From here, the railway joins the historic Arlbergbahn, completed in 1884 and centred on the 10,250-metre Arlberg Tunnel, whose construction claimed the lives of 92 workers. Emerging into Tyrol, the line passes St. Anton before descending towards Innsbruck, with the mountains closing in around the railway as it approaches the Tyrolean capital.

(O) Harbour of Lindau; (L) Lindau Train Station;
(T) Station signals; (B) The Rigoletto on Lake Constance

Mesopotamia Express *TÜRKIYE*

With its first services running in April 2024, the Mesopotamia Express is one of Türkiye's newest long-distance train routes. Taking 24 hours to trace the 1,050km from the capital Ankara to the Kurdish-majority city of Diyarbakır in the south, the train crosses the wide plains of central Anatolia before entering the more rugged landscapes of eastern Türkiye. Particularly worth exploring are the cities of Kayseri and Sivas, both home to Seljuk-era mosques and madrassahs carved with intricate stonework, as well as Elazığ – which boasts a splendid hilltop castle and one of Türkiye's oldest churches, dating back perhaps as far as 179 AD. The train terminates at Diyarbakır, where ancient churches and mosques nestle side-by-side with lively *caravanserais* and a dramatic black basalt castle.

(O) The Bürngüz Mosque; (T) Zerzevan Castle; (B) Mesopotamia Express

Northumberland Line

ENGLAND

Reopened to passengers after six decades, the Northumberland Line gives southeast Northumberland its railway back. The route runs between Newcastle and Ashington, via Manors, Northumberland Park, Seaton Delaval, Newsham, Blyth Bebside and Bedlington, making the full trip in around 35 minutes. Rather than spectacular scenery, the interest here comes from the places the railway reconnects: a region shaped by heavy industry and post-industrial change, with Newcastle at one end and the former mining communities of Northumberland at the other. It also puts the wild coast, country parks and industrial heritage of the county within easier reach. The route is a testament to what reopening a railway can do: changing daily movement, putting overlooked places back on the map and offering travellers a new way to explore the region.

(O) Foggy early morning commuter train on Northumberland Line; (L) Tyne Bridge; (R) Woodhorn Colliery Museum in Ashington

DE10 1104
ROMANTIC TRAIN
嵯峨野
SINCE 1991

Sagano Scenic Railway

JAPAN

Situated to the west of Kyoto, the Sagano Scenic Railway offers a short journey of around 7km, lasting just 25 minutes, which winds along the gorgeous Hozu River gorge to the nearby city of Kameoka. Originally built in the 1890s, the line became obsolete in 1989 when a quicker route was constructed, but it was quickly repurposed as a tourist train. It's now a popular attraction, particularly in spring, when the cherry blossom trees along the route bloom with bright pink blossom, and in autumn, when the leaves turn a rich orange and red. The journey also pairs naturally with the sights and activities of the wider area: the Arashiyama Bamboo Forest is close to the Saga end of the line, while Hozu River rafting offers a more adventurous way to experience the same valley.

(O) Sagano Romantic Train passing through a tunnel of cherry blossoms in Kyoto

Serra Verde Express *BRAZIL*

Deep in the heart of the Brazilian Atlantic Forest, the Serra Verde Express offers a vertiginous descent through one of the most biodiverse regions on the planet. Running from the high-altitude plateau of Curitiba to the colonial town of Morretes, the railway is a triumph of nineteenth-century engineering, clinging to the emerald-cloaked slopes of the Serra do Mar range. The journey is a sensory barrage of tropical humidity and dense foliage, punctuated by the thrill of crossing the São João Bridge – a narrow steel trestle spanning a deep, forested gorge that leaves passengers feeling as though they are floating above the canopy. Beyond the engineering, the route provides a vital glimpse into a rare ecosystem where hidden waterfalls tumble through the mist and bromeliads cling to every branch. It is a short but unforgettable route, capturing the humid, atmospheric transition from the cool highlands to the vibrant, coastal rhythms of southern Brazil.

(O) Serra Verde Express; (T) Mountain views from the train; (B) The historic centre of the city of Mortetes

Shrewsbury–Swansea Line *ENGLAND–WALES*

The Shrewsbury–Swansea route, better known as the Heart of Wales Line, is a slow 121-mile journey through the border country and hills of mid-Wales, linking market towns, remote valleys and small rural stations. From Shrewsbury's Grade II-listed Tudor Revival station, the train shares the main line past Church Stretton, with the Long Mynd to the west and Wenlock Edge to the east. At Craven Arms it turns onto single track, passing close to Stokesay Castle, then continuing through Bucknell and Knighton before crossing the 13-arch Knucklas Viaduct. The line reaches its highest point, around 299m above sea level, near Llangunllo before descending through Dolau, Pen-y-Bont and the spa town of Llandrindod Wells. With only a handful of trains each day, it remains a route for people willing to let the train decide the tempo.

(O) Shrewsbury Railway Station; (L) Stokesay Castle;
(T) Clocktower in Welsh market town of Knighton;
(B) Train leaving Shrewsbury Railway Station heading into Wales

Train des Pignes *FRANCE*

The Train des Pignes leaves from the unassuming Chemins de Fer de Provence station north of Nice Ville, then quickly exchanges the Riviera's glitz and polish for a more rugged Provence. At first the metre-gauge train clatters between buildings and level crossings, climbing through suburbs before turning north into the Var valley. After St-Martin-du-Var the valley closes in, the line following the river through the Défilé de Chaudan, where exposed rock strata and steep crags grow steadily more dramatic. Villars-sur-Var sits among vineyards, Touët-sur-Var clings to a rock face, and Puget-Théniers provides a market-town pause. By Entrevaux, with its fortified gateway and citadel, the journey has travelled a long way without ever needing to leave Provence.

(O) The fortifications of Entrevaux; (L) Train des Pignes in Provence; (R) Touët-sur-Var

Vall de Núria Rack Railway *SPAIN*

The Vall de Núria Rack Railway climbs from Ribes de Freser into a high Pyrenean valley that cannot be reached by road, a fact that immediately gives the journey a sense of escape. Known in Catalan as the Cremallera de Núria, the rack railway was built to provide access to the sanctuary and valley beyond the roadless upper reaches of the Ter Valley. As it climbs, the valley tightens, the air cools and the landscape moves from village foothills into mountain pasture and rocky slopes. Núria itself, with its sanctuary, lake and surrounding walking country, has the contained atmosphere of a place shaped by geography as much as tourism. With no road into the upper valley, the train carries you steadily from the foothills into Núria, following the narrowing valley as the landscape becomes increasingly wild.

(O) Train gliding through Vall de Núria; (L) Scenic Vall de Núria; (T) Ribes de Freser Station; (B) View from the driver cab of a narrow gauge railway in Vall de Núria

Venice–Zagreb *ITALY–SLOVENIA–CROATIA*

The Venice–Zagreb journey begins with one of Europe's great railway departures, leaving Santa Lucia station across the causeway over the Venetian Lagoon, with water stretching away on both sides of the track. For the more rewarding itinerary, change at Gorizia and Jesenice to follow the Bohinj Railway through Slovenia. From Nova Gorica the line crosses the Soča on the 219.7m Solkan Bridge, built from 4,500 stone blocks, then follows the Soča, Idrijca and Bača valleys before entering the 6.3km Bohinj Tunnel. Lake Bled appears near Bled Jezero, then Ljubljana gives the journey a compact, café-lined pause. South of the Slovenian capital, the railway follows the Sava through curves, tunnels and deep cuttings before crossing at Dobova and approaching Zagreb through fields, villages and the edges of the modern Croatian capital.

(O) Railway leading to Venice; (T) Solkan Bridge; (B) Lake Bled

Luxury & Legendary Trains

Luxury trains pair remarkable landscapes with a style of travel that recalls the golden age of rail. Behind polished timber, brass fittings and elegantly laid dining tables, they cross deserts, mountains, jungle and high plains in exceptional comfort. Some were created for maharajas, viceroys and royalty, while others have been reimagined as rolling hotels offering refined service through some of the world's most spectacular scenery.

Andean Explorer *PERU*

(T) Andean Explorer crossing the Peruvian Andes

Traversing the high plains of southern Peru, the Andean Explorer combines luxurious accommodation with one of South America's most spectacular rail journeys. One of the world's highest sleeper trains, it crosses the Altiplano, where snow-capped peaks, broad grasslands and herds of alpacas dominate the landscape. Large observation areas and elegant interiors inspired by Andean craftsmanship encourage passengers to appreciate the scenery rather than rush through it. Depending on the itinerary, the route links Cusco, Lake Titicaca and Arequipa, revealing high mountain passes, volcanic landscapes and immense open plateaux. It is a journey through one of the world's highest inhabited landscapes, with vast skies, distant mountains and long stretches of open country along the way.

Belmond Hiram Bingham *PERU*

Named after the explorer who brought Machu Picchu to international attention, the Belmond Hiram Bingham is one of South America's finest luxury trains, combining the romance of classic rail travel with an exceptional journey through the Peruvian Andes. Departing from Cusco, its elegant Pullman-style carriages wind through the Sacred Valley, following the Urubamba River past cultivated terraces, traditional mountain villages and dramatic, steep-sided Andean slopes. The journey is as much about the experience on board as the scenery beyond the windows, with beautifully presented dining, live Peruvian music and attentive service. As the train approaches Aguas Calientes, the landscape becomes more secluded and atmospheric, with lush vegetation and cloud-forested peaks signalling the proximity of Machu Picchu. Arriving at the gateway to the ancient citadel, the Hiram Bingham provides a memorable introduction to one of the world's most celebrated archaeological sites.

(O) Belmond Hiram Bigham passing through the Sacred Valley; (L) Train passing through the Peruvian Andes; (T) Live Peruvian music on board; (B) Luxury restaurant car

Belmond Royal Scotsman

SCOTLAND

The Belmond Royal Scotsman turns Highland rail travel into a polished world of fine dining, Champagne and Edwardian-style comfort. Since its inaugural run in 1985, the train has carried a small number of guests from Edinburgh Waverley in purple-liveried carriages, with a kilted bagpiper, an Observation Car and a Dior Spa carriage. The experience could easily feel overdone were the landscapes less commanding. On the West Highland Line, Loch Long, Loch Lomond and Rannoch Moor supply the first sweep of mountains, lochs and birch woods. At Kyle of Lochalsh, the Isle of Skye comes within reach, while Eilean Donan, Ben Nevis, the Caledonian Canal and Dalmore Distillery add a castle, mountain, canal and whisky into the itinerary before the train rolls back towards Edinburgh across the Forth Railway Bridge.

(O) Belmond Royal Scotsman crossing the Glenfinnan Viaduct; (L) Forth Bridge; (R) Luxury cabin onboard the Belmond Royal Scotsman

Blue Train *SOUTH AFRICA*

Running between the high-veld of Pretoria and Cape Town's coast, South Africa's Blue Train has defined luxury rail travel for nearly a century. The journey is a study in shifting perspectives, carrying passengers from the administrative heart of the north through the haunting, arid expanse of the Great Karoo, where the vast sky meets a flat, ancient horizon. Within the train's mahogany-paneled suites, the atmosphere is one of timeless refinement, punctuated by the ritual of high tea and the rhythmic clink of crystal in the lounge car. As the route concludes with a dramatic descent through the lush Winelands toward the looming silhouette of Table Mountain, the experience solidifies its reputation not just as a mode of transport, but as a grand, slow-motion celebration of the diverse South African landscape.

(O) The Blue Train crossing the Karoo; (T) Luxury sleeping quarters; (B) First-class service on board The Blue Train

E&O

Eastern & Oriental Express

SINGAPORE–MALAYSIA

Employing 1970s Japanese rolling stock, given an elegant old-world cladding with wooden inlay work and featuring Thai and Malay motifs, the Eastern & Oriental Express offers a delightful slow-travel route from Singapore to Kuala Lumpur. Journeys take four days and involve a variety of excursions, which include wildlife-spotting in Taman Nagara National Park and guided tours to the colonial settlement of Georgetown. Spending time on the train is an experience in itself: the sleeping cars are luxurious, the food in the opulent dining car is first class, and there's even an on-board spa. Not least, an observation deck at the back of the train allows passengers to make the most of the passing scenery.

(O) Eastern & Oriental Express staff welcoming passengers onboard

RAKESH

Maharajas' Express *INDIA*

The Maharajas' Express is India's premier luxury train, combining opulent accommodation with journeys through some of the country's most celebrated landscapes, historic cities and cultural landmarks. Introduced in 2010, it offers several itineraries linking destinations such as Agra, Jaipur, Jodhpur, Varanasi and Ranthambore National Park, allowing travellers to experience a broad cross-section of northern India in a single journey. The train's elegant cabins, fine dining and attentive service evoke the grandeur of a bygone era of royal travel, while spacious interiors and carefully considered details create an atmosphere of understated luxury. Beyond the train itself, each itinerary reveals a different side of India, from the Mughal splendour of Agra and the colourful palaces of Rajasthan to desert forts, sacred rivers and wildlife reserves. More than simply a luxurious way to travel, the Maharajas' Express offers a richly varied introduction to the history, culture, architecture and landscapes of northern India.

(O) Maharajas Express lounge bar; (T) Deluxe cabin; (B) Luxury dining onboard

Palace ON Wheels INDIA

(T) Luxury cabin onboard the Palace on Wheels

The Palace on Wheels is one of India's classic luxury trains, recreating the elegance and grandeur of the royal rail journeys once associated with the princely states of Rajasthan. Richly decorated cabins, ornate dining cars and attentive service provide a fitting setting for a week-long circuit from Delhi through some of northern India's most celebrated historic cities and cultural landmarks. The itinerary includes Jaipur, Jaisalmer, Jodhpur and Udaipur before concluding at the Taj Mahal in Agra, bringing together desert landscapes, imposing hill forts, elaborate palaces and Mughal architecture in a single journey. Between visits, passengers return to the comfort of the train, where beautifully appointed interiors and fine dining create a sense of travelling in a bygone era. More than a means of travel, the Palace on Wheels makes the journey itself part of the experience, offering a distinctive way to discover the history and splendour of Rajasthan and northern India.

PeruRail Titicaca Train

PERU

The PeruRail Titicaca Train links the colonial city of Cusco with Puno on the shores of Lake Titicaca, crossing one of the highest railways in South America and offering a spectacular journey through the Peruvian Andes. Climbing steadily to La Raya Pass at 4,319m, the route leaves cultivated Andean valleys behind for the vast open landscapes of the Altiplano, where grazing alpacas and vicuñas are scattered across high mountain grasslands beneath snow-capped peaks. The open-air observation car provides uninterrupted views of this remarkable scenery, while the train's elegant interiors and dining carriage recall the classic age of rail travel. By the time the journey reaches Lake Titicaca, the world's highest navigable lake, it has revealed one of the Andes' most distinctive landscapes, where immense skies and broad plateaux stretch to every horizon.

(O) PeruRail Titicaca Train from Cusco to Puno; (L) Luxury dining car; (T) PeruRail Titicaca Train; (B) La Raya Railway Station

Rovos Rail *SOUTH AFRICA*

Rovos Rail is one of the world's finest luxury trains, combining the atmosphere of the golden age of rail travel with the changing landscapes of South Africa. Departing from its private station at Capital Park in Pretoria, the wood-panelled carriages cross the highveld to Kimberley before continuing through the wide open spaces of the Great Karoo towards Cape Town. Life on board follows an elegant, relaxed rhythm, with fine dining, attentive service and generous observation areas encouraging passengers to appreciate the journey as much as the destinations. The open-air observation balcony is one of the train's defining features, allowing the landscapes, wildlife and vast skies of southern Africa to be experienced without interruption. The approach to Cape Town, with Table Mountain rising above the city, provides a fitting conclusion to one of the world's great luxury rail journeys.

(O) Luxury dining car (T) Observation car; (B) Rovos Rail travelling through the Langeberg Valley

Seven Stars *IN* Kyushu *JAPAN*

Japan's first luxury sleeper train, the Seven Stars in Kyushu, began operation in 2013. Built around the symbolism of the number seven, the train has seven cars and itineraries designed to reveal Kyushu through its history, cuisine, nature, hot springs, craftsmanship and railway heritage. Starting from Hakata, in Fukuoka, journeys vary in length and destination, but all explore the island's diverse landscapes, from volcanic mountains and fertile plains to rugged coastlines and forested valleys. Inside, the train draws directly on Kyushu's craft traditions, with polished wood, traditional motifs and fittings made by local artisans used throughout the restaurant car, saloon and suites. The result is an interior that reflects the island's design heritage as closely as the journeys reflect its landscapes.

(O) Seven Stars in Kyushu in spring; (T) Scenes of paddy fields and mountains onboard the Seven Stars; (B) Luxury cabin

Twilight Express Mizukaze *JAPAN*

Japan's railways are usually about speed and pinpoint efficiency, but the Twilight Express Mizukaze makes a persuasive case for slowing right down. Running between Kyoto or Osaka and Shimonoseki, the train follows two-day itineraries that combine overnight travel with stops at some of western Honshū's best-known sights. Along the way are Onomichi, with its temple-dotted hillsides, Miyajima rising from the Seto Inland Sea, the historic canals of Kurashiki and the celebrated bridge at Iwakuni. On board, the sense of place continues through refined interiors, attentive service and menus inspired by the produce and culinary traditions of western Japan. With the Seto Inland Sea, castle towns and wooded hills unfolding beyond the windows, the train turns a route between major destinations into a slower exploration of western Japan.

(O) Onomichi city; (L) Itsukushima Torii Gate, Miyajima Island; (R) Twilight Express Mizukaze

VENICE
SIMPLON
ORIENT-EXPRESS
N°

Venice Simplon-Orient-Express

EUROPE

Few trains carry such a burden of myth as the Venice Simplon-Orient-Express. Its history can be traced back to the inaugural Orient Express of 1883, when passengers left Paris bound for Constantinople, continuing by ferry, train and steamship because the railway was not yet complete. The modern VSOE is a revival rather than a direct continuation, relaunched in 1982 after James B. Sherwood located and painstakingly restored a collection of 1920s Wagons-Lits and Pullman cars. Today, operated by Belmond, the experience begins with liveried stewards, beautifully restored sleeping cars, intricate marquetry, Lalique glass and cocktails in Bar Car 3674, recreated from a 1931 restaurant car. New itineraries, including a route between Paris and the Amalfi Coast, demonstrate that the Venice Simplon-Orient-Express continues to evolve while preserving the elegance and craftsmanship that made it one of the world's most celebrated trains.

(O) Venice Simplon-Orient-Express cabin steward waiting for guests

Publishing information

The World by Train • 100 Legendary Railway Journeys
Editor: Beth Williams
Proofreader: Kate Drynan
Writers: Owen Morton & Robert Savage
Designer: Michał Ptasznik
Picture Editor: Piotr Kala
Picture Manager: Tom Smyth
Production Operations Manager: Katie Bennett
Publishing Technology Manager: Rebeka Davies
Head of Publishing: Sarah Clark

Our selection
The World by Train • 100 Legendary Railway Journeys offers our curation of the most exceptional destinations in the world, with content selected from Rough Guides, plus original content by Owen Morton and Robert Savage.

First Edition 2026

ISBN: 9781835296509

Printed by Finidr in Czech Republic

A catalogue record for this book is available from the British Library.

MIX
Paper | Supporting responsible forestry
FSC www.fsc.org FSC® C014138

DISTRIBUTION
UK, Ireland and Europe
Apa Publications (UK) Ltd; mail@roughguides.com
United States and Canada
Two Rivers; ips@ ingramcontent.com
Australia and New Zealand
Woodslane; info@woodslane.com.au
Worldwide
Apa Publications (UK) Ltd; mail@roughguides.com

SPECIAL SALES, CONTENT LICENSING AND COPUBLISHING
Rough Guides can be purchased in bulk quantities at discounted prices. We can create special editions, personalized jackets and corporate imprints tailored to your needs.
mail@roughguides.com; http://roughguides.com

EU REPRESENTATIVE
LOGOS EUROPE, 9 rue Nicolas Poussin, 17000, LA ROCHELLE, France
Contact@logoseurope.eu; +33 (0) 667937378

Photo credits

All images Shutterstock except:
Alamy 16, 26, 44, 52, 82/83, 86, 108, 113T, 157T, 228, 240/241
Andrew Gregory/Journey Beyond Group 136/137
Belmond 220, 221BL, 221TR, 223R, 226/227, 242/243
Cruise Train Seven Stars in Kyushu (JR Kyushu) 236, 237B, 237T
khws4v1/Flickr under CC BY 2.0 license 239R
Loco Steve/Flickr under CC BY-SA 4.0 license 48
Lyndie Pavier Photography/Rovos Rail 107TR
Maharaja's Express 229T
Matt Crossick/Belmond 218/219
Rovos Rail 107BR, 216, 234, 235B, 235T
Sanjeev Verma Photography 229B

Cover credit: The Bernina Express in Switzerland **iStock**

Caption key
(L) = left
(R) = right
(T) = top
(B) = bottom
(O) = opposite

THE **world**
IS **waiting**

Make the **legend**
your own

山村
TRAIN CREW